Death Sentences

ALSO BY TOBY OLSON

POETRY
We are the fire: a selection of poems
Unfinished Building
Human Nature
Darklight*

FICTION
The Life of Jesus
Seaview
The Woman Who Escaped From Shame
Utah
Dorit in Lesbos
At Sea
Write Letter to Billy
The Blond Box
The Bitter Half
Tampico

MEMOIR
The Other Woman*

Shearsman titles

Toby Olson

Death Sentences

Shearsman Books

First published in the United Kingdom in 2019 by
Shearsman Books
50 Westons Hill Drive
Emersons Green
BRISTOL
BS16 7DF

Shearsman Books Ltd Registered Office
30–31 St. James Place, Mangotsfield, Bristol BS16 9JB
(this address not for correspondence)

www.shearsman.com

ISBN 978-1-84861-668-4

ACKNOWLEDGEMENTS
Some of these poems have appeared in *Conjunctions, Dispatches From
The Poetry Wars, Fiction International, Golden Handcuffs Review* and
The Anthology of World Poetry of the 21ˢᵗ Century, Vol. 10.

Contents

Inspiration		9
Standard 18: There Will Never Be Another You		10
Death Sentences		15
The Red Ribbon		22
Flowers		
	1 New Guinea Impatiens	25
	2 Tulip Feeder	26
	3 Lantana	27
	4 A Rose	28
	5 Funereal Flowers	29
	6 The Wrist Corsage, A Memory	31
	7 The Yellow Chalice Vine	32
	8 Pansies	35
	9 Oldfield Toadflax	36
	10 That Begonia	37
	11 Still Life with Geranium	39
	12 Flower Children	40
I Don't Know		42
After the Storm		49
After the Photograph		50
After the Concert		51
After Long Silence		52
After the Wedding		53
After the Fall		54
After Divorce		55
After Angelica Waiting		56
After Longstanding		57
After Lingering Illness		58
After Death		59
Afterwards		60
I've Lost My Whistle		61
Disturbed		63
A Wink and a Nod		70

Child Lost in the Forest 72
Etudes 76
That Way 83
The Meal 85

For Miriam

forever

Inspiration

The cat is out of the bag,
and the music is Bill Evans, not the trio,
but alone.

Somewhere along the line,
under the strains
      of *My Foolish Heart,*
the people in this room
are filled with ideas.

There is no room,
and there are no people.

This is my inspiration.
There is only Bill Evans.

Standard-18,
There Will Never Be Another You

How quickly does the weight of time come down upon us.
Foreclosure:
      Christmas, Passover, Independence,
and roses
wilting in the pot you may have placed for them,
the various frustrated markers.

And long gone too
the freshness of things discovered:
      the texture of your hair,
your beautiful toes,
my finger pressed in the wetness of your arm pit.

What is romance?
Outside
the winter wind is cautionary
snow flakes into wet drops on the window.
      Soon the shovel, the broom,
those thoughts of you while digging
in a daze.

And yet a chickadee, shivering on the feeder, alert,
his last dance
to music I had thought to cling to,
      Keith Jarrett's fingers in "My Old Flame,"
as if the keys were lips,
      other songs, another fall,
maybe another spring.

Love is the answer:
        the gone ones answering
in the earth's ripening,
should spring
ever come to this troubled mind,
should the living forget those haunted
images of the dead,
so the dead might live in the common memory.

Last week, justice was in the offing.
I aimed to shoot the rabbit
but missed him.
        He had chewed at your flowers,
his nature.
Only in mistaken weaponry was he spared.

What is death?
        What is the nature
of these endings?
The flowers multiply before wilting
as do the rabbits.

Undeterred:
That waking dream
        of a delicate young man in glasses
in uniform, in book camp, and the bastard
Chief Petty Officer
finding a bit of soap in one ear.
He removed it brutality with a pencil,
        then forced him into the shower
in his clothing, his glasses, in front of all of us.
He wept then, water soaking his uniform,
        mingling with tears on his dignified face.
He had lost the terms of his life.
He had lost his life.

Would that I was older then,
and had this rifle.

Nights like this:
I'll be standing there with someone new,
        threads of a silken scarf in memory in my fingers,
other lips that I might kiss.
Our thrill is gone.

Maudlin:
The books you gave me,
        many unread. Your various accomplishments
seen but unseen.

        And in our moment of parting
you were alone in the bed
six feet away.
You were always alone.

So much sabotage
        on our long road home:
women and drink, my failings, my insanity.
I would ask for a moment of forgiveness.
Too late. At the end
        you didn't know my name.
Who was I then?

There's a poem in here somewhere,
a kind of fiction that I remember
or imagine,
visiting Walter's farm.

Dinner and talk, fine wine,
        and in the morning

out in the yard, close to the silo,
with the shotgun.

"Too many pigeons."
        Doing something destructive?
I don't remember.

I raised the gun awkwardly
into the sky.
Three pigeons fell to the ground,
two dead, one
        struggling to leave this planet,
there
in the scatter of hay and straw.

"You have to kill her," Walter said.
"It's humane."

I couldn't do it. The passage
        would be her own,
as yours was.

That night I returned to the pigeon's resting place,
then went to my bed in the old farm house.
I slept the sleep of a wanderer.

About pigeons and rabbits, a guy in a shower,
a chickadee, the tassels on your hat,
a rifle and a shotgun.
        About life and death, about dreaming,
about the picture of you with your new bicycle,
about memory:
        the dead's messages
written into the skins of the living.

And the last story:

In the early morning,
        before the living rose up,
I carried you to the car,
            then drove to the cemetery.

The place was empty,
but for the birds,
        those mourning doves
you so loved.

And in the earth,
in front of the stone marker
upon which your name was carved,
        I dug a deep hole
and buried your ashes
among tree roots and stones.

You were not there.

Death Sentences

1

Stumbled among stones until
toes wetted in surf's gentle wash
having come here to the edge
where pipers plow with pointed beaks
only to dash away
leaving momentary excavations
that pucker then disappear
as memory holes
in which past life might live
and die as all things possible
become nothing
here at the end of land
just inches beyond stones that were
Flint Granite Quartz and Glass.

2

Subdued danger of the brown-tale rash
and clothing for outside adventure
otherwise luxurious living
as days turn into years
and months are theatrical characters
whose presence is accusing every day
although unbidden
in this crucible that limps along
until the old man swallows up the young
and he who was a fraud and fake
discovers his flagrant character
too late for correction
out on the porch in perfect weather
where he sits and weeps.

3

What price vocabulary of the living world
few names for flowers trees and dogs
that bloom and move so certainly
until windy weather cars or saws possess them
lest they stay and become a prophecy
of what's to come
days without end of gorgeous weather
which the moved along will not savor
here in the pleasure of trials and tribulations
as the mystery train travels
into uncertain futures
and even the sick at heart
look out the window to see
rows of lilacs and coreopsis blooming.

4

In Truro when the time was ripe
which is a metaphor
including all passengers
even those blinded by ambition
there was a house set against storm
in which a woman once lived
then died leaving parcels of her life behind
in bags that relatives sorted
in preparation for a yard sale
of worn cutlery and dishes
dresses and furniture
and jewelry impressed with her scent
who had lived in the way we all live
and will leave in the same way too.

5

Back to the sea
where they fish in sunset
and never see it for what it is
clock of the earth's turning
a possible message
for those facing into the glow
who are struck blind when they turn
until their world comes into focus
transient and then fixed
for the time being
all this before the inevitability beckons
and legs start failing
even when standing still while fishing
hauling up dark bottom dwellers.

6

They who are here are no longer here
yet those who are gone
are still truculent after passage
into cocoons in memory's storage
where light footed and dancing
they break through that webbing
and after hours of drinking
in fake celebration
do the living stumble intoxicated
into their beds and the nightly
death sleep which presages
until they rise up in the morning
the rot of night in their nostrils
empty of memory.

7

Much of the dark preaching goes unnoticed
by the fidgeting children
pew locked and longing
before the sepulcher teaching and the threats
while those who know better are praying
for the eternal
that is already there
outside these confines
in trees and sun and ever changing grasses
beside the concrete parking lot and the cars
that will in time
enter the living earth
as will all people and this steeple
when preaching is forgotten.

8

Back to the sea again those gentle swells
upon which gulls sit
and wreckage washes up to be examined
so that the distant past might live again
in reconstructions of the sailors' mess
a wheel house and old coins
whose value is found in imprints
of kings and monarchs from foreign places
that no longer exist
but in the fascination for a cleansing
by retrogression that will turn the clocks back
and the dead will become the living
though in the same frustrations
that the living now inhabit.

9

X my only love
harken back to sea wrack
in childhood on these beaches
where plovers still run and fishermen
cast out their plugs that search
in deep waters for a kind of offering
so that families might devour the sacraments
brought up
and you left the table
hungry for ice cream
melting into death on your fingers
and all your friend are running forward
or away as sun sinks
and the moon rises.

10

A story in which there are no characters
but for the sun's wash on everything
that is not human
but can act that way in yucca
dipping its long spear as if nodding
and the small nest the snake approaches
with an attention
humans might mimic in metaphor
seeing the world from the ground up
to avoid the dying pines and oaks
that will in time fall away
as what is now becomes a desert
and all that seemed possible has its ending
here there or anywhere.

11

When at times our Sunday best is not enough
and guarded under raiments
of personality we go unnoticed
at church banquets and dancing frenzy
in order to find a presentation of the living
where constant motion forestalls the peaceful ending
that dark promise
and as clothing wears and we under it
find resignation of peaceful stillness
in which solitude in vacant eyes
might understand the final closure
banishing ego
until in that unexpected rattle
everything is left behind for the others.

12

Another story of a man this time
who in the metaphor is less than a stick figure
though bound over for autopsy
in a well lighted room
smelling of gentle chemicals
while relatives upstairs are waiting
to see him as he was in life
and all in the vibrant world
speak the uniqueness of this passage
yet doors stand open
beyond which their endings beckon
even as the deliriums of action
deny its inevitable coming and the flowers
around the casket begin to stink.

13

Ah yes the flowers the trees the birds
and the sea under which and above
uncounted time keeps passing
leaving the dead behind and forgotten
until there is none left for memory
though not yet not yet
for the fishermen still face the sea
and Caroline remains lascivious there
awaiting upon a satisfaction
that as with all else is transitory
while fish hang dead on the line
and birds fly into glass
blocking a passage
similar to the ones we think protect us.

14

Having come now to an ending
though not the end
that has no future beginnings
even in bacteria
that float unseen on the waves' surface
and presages nothing
in a journey on that sea always returned to
as if it were some message
speaking of life's continuance eternally
above remnants of a sunken past forgotten
when what is remembered
has no living vessel to contain it
even death becomes silent
and tongues are rotten in the mouth.

The Red Ribbon

1

The red ribbon is tied in her hair,
and it celebrates her hair,
blond, a quarter inch of black at the roots,
and she thinks of the President's madness
and that quarter inch
of the real emerging. What can she do?
He waits at the edge of the wood, and she
in her plain country shift
is ready to get rid of all thoughts of
presidents and houses and senates,
since her head is filled with congress,
and the tales of the red ribbon
are bouncing as she moves quickly toward him
in the failing light.

2

Everybody fancies the ribbon,
it's red with gold thread
      stitched in along its borders
and there's an emblem.
Perhaps the rich will conspire,
anything to get it.
Yet it is only a ribbon and not currency
though that is the way the rich see it.
Money, money, money,
      there's nothing like it!
It's only a ribbon, and yet
it is beautiful and not precious,
but like the man said, "Business is business,
but love is bullshit."

3

The document is closed with a red ribbon
that the President struggles to untie,
then he gets it
and all in the small audience applaud.
With a flourish, he signs it
      then holds it up
turning as if it were some holy text.
Then all applaud again.
Birds chirp in the White House trees.
Chipmunks settle down
      in holes in the lawn.
Who is the first lady?
The only thing in the room
that seem real is the red ribbon.

4

She gave him a red ribbon
that he didn't want,
then insisted that he snake it
      through his belt loops
and tie it in the front.
This was just the beginning,
for she was foolish and insistent,
and he was her sap.
Ribbons are without power
to hold pants up,
thus does he dance away
covering his crotch.
She wont quit.
It's *her* ribbon. He's *hers.*

5

The red ribbon is torn from the gift
of the unknown anticipated
by the one who leans forward
a flower in her hair
wondering what it could be
as the giver sweats in his own anticipation:
will she like it, will she demure?
Does it matter what the box contains?
Some say it's the thought that counts.
She is not thinking, but wishing
to like anything given by him.
There's a good deal of hesitation.
Open the damned box!
She toys with the ribbon.

6

The red ribbon is only a ribbon
until it stands for something:
    solidarity, the battle against disease,
blood of course and even stroke.
The red ribbon has no power,
yet it is powerful when worn be people
in certain groups, even by those
not on the barricades, but in offices,
    writing changes to various regulations,
the backbone of movements.
The official sits at his desk.
He is assaulted by paper, and the red ribbon
    dances on the heads
of the thousands
gathered for change.

Flowers

1 New Guinea Impatiens

I wonder if in New Guinea they are impatient,
as we are: all those languages, sharp and melodious,
on the streets of Los Angeles, and tribes conversing
in Mount Hagen and the Gulf villages.
    Impatient for roasted pig, dance costumes,
the Singing Dog. Impatient for a change in scenery,
a trip at least to Bakersfield,
a different life.

Flowers ring our East Coast properties
and are not there by happenstance.
    Each choosing, each careful planting,
each impatient for its blooming.

The times are hard in Massachusetts, New York City,
as they might well be in New Guinea and Los Angeles,
and yet there is certainly dancing and singing, each song
a flower
parceled out in a new beginning.

I will press my face into their moist blossoming.
All our flowers, as well as those in New Guinea,
are sexual.

Henceforth, I will be singing and will not be impatient.
These flowers were purchased
for what seems now
a song.

2 Tulip Feeder

Humming birds on the glass feeder
shaped like a tulip.
> They suck up the nectar,
and spill drops of sugar

> on the grass below, the flowers below,
the worm below, and the chipmunk:
all there or coming there
for nourishment.

Now suddenly do we discover
the snake
> in this polluted grass,
who climbs the pole after a mouth full.

Humming birds are fragile.
Thus are they swift, and only
vulnerable at rest,
but for the hawk's
death strike.

This tulip is made of glass
and will not grow old and die,
as the real tulips will.

These humming birds will grow old and die,
as will this grass, the chipmunk,
the snake.

Below this atmosphere, the polluted earth.
It too might die, as will we,
eventually. The worm will search and find us all
and is immortal.

3 Lantana

Haunted lantana
unpruned, your green vines
      reaching out for another place,
a life
in which your star clusters-
yellow, purple, red, bandana cherry
and Carlos, golden Christine
      and violet—
are properly tended by someone
other than me,

      that one in winter, the lazy bum,
who has left you there to wither
into skeleton grey stalks
      as in movies or paintings where,
unbeknownst to the heroine,
fairies dance among rot
near a marsh in England.

I have no time for flowers,
and they have little time for me.

Yet your beauty is remarked,
if only in passing,
      when you reach to touch
my starboard leg
your radiation blossoms rustbit
for lack of water.

And so I water you and wait
for cherry sunrise to return again.

4 A Rose

Who gives a rose with care for satisfaction,
but pathetically, a single stem, denuded
of its guarding thorns,
lest they prick the lover's palm,
his could be the stupid music of a love
for she who sticks it in a narrow fluted vase
and thus forgets it, until
she hears a knocking at the door
and thinks "it's him,
come for some reward"
that will not be given,
but for an enigmatic smile,
and "thank you for that lovely flower"
that in the meantime has blossomed,
then faded
and dropped its fleshy red petals
to form a sad circle on the glass table
out of sight.

5 Funereal Flowers

Nobody should lie among gladiolus, standing
      in tall wicker at the quilting of his new home.
Character, moral integrity, sayeth the florist
garnering wealth.

Yet the mourners admire them, and the white lilies
      [innocence restored to the departed soul]
and the red roses [grief and sorrow, and courage too].
         And their various scents, blossoming, pollen
and lantana, and the memory of bees buzzing and sucking nectar
They cannot see the dead from their seats.

All summer long, chrysanthemums [death
and grieving] and white carnations.
All these signature values imagined by florists.

The bride stands at the window.

Where is the flower girl, the ring bearer?
Where is the groom?
Yet this is a marriage of worlds
and the transit between them,
and flowers stir in the breeze
provided by the air conditioner.

No one is at peace in his casket,
his new home.
Memories of childhood, of wild flowers
presented to his bride at a similar altar,
memories of last week,
all gone, but for the transit.

Before the lid closes,
before the bearers move to their stations,
before the florist counts his money,
        and before the staged ceremony comes
to it's theatrical end,
the dead shall rise up from his casket,
and his body
or at least his soul, or in the imagination,
shall walk out into the summer sunset,
followed by the scent of flowers.

6 The Wrist Corsage, A Memory

Brilliant pink cloth flowers,
feathered wrist corsage,
fancy in its old conservative way.

It's the homecoming dance,
pink carnations
in a little white box
held awkwardly at his hip.

"Here," he says
and hands it over,
in memory.

She's forgotten his tie,
his awkward smile,
his father's car.

Once upon a time,
long gone.

She thinks of the little box,
his crisp white cuff,
that awkwardness in the dancing.

She's forgotten his name, yet remembers
that fleeting kiss,
his lack of imagination with flowers.

7 The Yellow Chalice Vine

"Let's go to college," Ollie said.
Corpus Christi, the navy,
1960,
      but I was thinking of Mary Grace
naked in the placid surf,
          flowers in her hair,
though on the Gulf the Portugese man-of-war
were drifting in.

"Why not," I said,
      our thoughts drifting too,
heading for California.

Two young guys,
no real passions in our eyes,
      but wonderment of where to go,
         what to do.
We should make plans, I thought,
but there, again, was Mary Grace.

A late fall afternoon on Padre Island,
      almost empty in those days,
we walked along the beach,
then headed inland
         —low, gentle, dunes—
and came upon a stand of pine,
a little forest here
      in Texas,
—only sixty yards square—
where we had spent a year and more
without sufficiency,
         but for those flowers

in the women's hair
we thought to love
and leave.

I had not seen the character in trees.
I was bewildered,
        always looking inward,
but these branches were skirts
falling over one another,
                long green candle fingers
hung from hidden hands,
close to brushing the sandy ground.

Then came upon a small clearing in this fiction
and discovered the trunk
            of a dead tree, severed
to a small man's height
        and slightly leaning
under the encircling weight of the Chalice Vine,
its glossy foliage
and its aphrodisiac flowers, large yellow petals
                curling back and changing
to become bright gold in their opening.

This is the tree of the wind, Kieli,
        god of the wind and black magic.

Thick vines encircled the body of the dead tree,
snaked under arms,
between legs,
        stroking a cheek, a neck,
all hidden beneath the foliage of vines and leaves.
A flower had opened near the leaning tree's head.
Its petals brushed the bark, his shadowy face.

The Chalice Vine is erotic,
its embrace the embrace of sexual love,
          but also love itself in sex
and also life.

I thought I saw the dead tree shudder
in the vague scent of coconut.

          "Let's go to college."
Ollie spoke in a laughing whisper,
breaking the spell.

We turned away.

The flowers seemed to be watching us,
burning their presence
into the backs of our heads.

These were the Cups of Gold.

8 Pansies

They call you a pansy,
and I, for one, am watching
your delicate movements,
      dancing around the field,
never footing the ball
or the other players.

Pansies: the color in the core,
      shape of an eagle landing,
a hairy old man's face,
as in a coven,
a crowd of dogs watching.

The field is surrounded
      by pansies, a rainbow,
and the pink rosie posies
stand among them, on long green stems.

And you, my dear child,
are moving
within that encircling.
      It's only a game after all,
these laughing insults.

And at the intermission,
or the time out, or at half time,
      you are prancing, smiling,
as you move to the sideline,
a pansy.

It doesn't matter to me
if you are a boy
or a girl.

9 Oldfield Toadflax

Skinny as you are with your blue hats
I love you,

which to some may well be a sin,
give gay marriage
and the domino effect:

marriage to cats and chickens, to a gold fish,
a sparrow hawk, a brother,
and of course dogs and hogs.

But flowers are not such fools,
their beauty your beauty,
that of feral, vegetative music.

Some call you a weed even in
your blooming.
Yet you are gay, swaying,
nodding in the breeze.

10 That Begonia

The big oak is dropping its acorns
that ping among withered leaves on the little deck
Larry and I constructed
long ago,
          which time is,
in the way of years,
gone now, here in the early fall in North Truro.

Nothing much:
these skeletal trees, these clapboards
turning grey, this world of no distinguishing color.

And yet, in a brown ceramic pot at the deck's edge,
          the bright red Switzerland begonia,
its waxen, veined and pointed green leaves
there to dress that blooming,
                    flowers whose petals fold and gather
into a tight fleshy center
that seems almost edible,
as red as any bloody satisfaction.

We round the house
and set out on the narrow road
that runs between endless fields
of withered corn, their last cobs fallen,
as they soon will, as far as the eye can see.

Abandoned cars in weeds at the road side,
          rusted and burned out.
Flowers that thrived in passenger seats
are wilted now.
                    The sky is dark, heavy black clouds
full of cold rain.

We hear the quiet moan of a few mourning doves,
invisible among the stalks.

This is not Truro,
or anywhere, though it too seems lifeless.

As fall comes on,
I've been thinking about my life,
my losses,
my lover and my friends.
And I've been thinking too about that begonia.

It was so red!

11 Still Life with Geranium

A dead duck, a ham sandwich, a trout,
      and to the left a dim candle.
On the far right,
a rifle, a fishing pole.

In the center all is uncertain,
as are the passing days,
      but for this uncommon geranium,
the order of a singular flowering,
limp, purple petals,
black business at the core.

The duck will not fade away.
      The sandwich will not be eaten.
The trout will not decay.

But the geranium, like all flowers,
will bow to the inevitable
leaving the center of the still life vacant.

12 Flower Children

Puberty will not harm them.
      Sex will not harm them.
The State will not prevail against them.
Harmony will protect them.

Tellytubbies'
      heads bristling with clover,
sunflowers, lavender, mushrooms,
even miniature pine trees,
cherries.

They will be dancing,
the youth of a nation comes forward,
      harmless, in subtle revolt.
The innocence of childhood is within them.
All will be well.

Flower Children
walking the streets of Beijing,
      teenagers, some a little older,
some shy.
Even in the rain, in humidity, in storm,
      no appeasement, luxury, no aggression.
They are crowned, casual.
They pace the earth, which is sidewalks,
streets, school halls, parks.

I saw them from a dark doorway and laughed,
and they laughed too, then spoke to one another,
      looked into shop windows, bodegas,
mirrors.
Flowers were growing from their heads.

Maturity will not harm them.
      Singularity will not harm them.
The state will not prevail against them.
Harmony will protect them.

"Let one hundred flowers bloom!"

I Don't Know

1

Shovels scrape on the sidewalks
while it's still snowing
        and wind is blowing the drifts
back over the cleared spaces
to again institute that silence provided
in winter when snowy weather
covers all the sins of frustrated cracked streets
that are evidence of a government
without will or money
and I don't know
what to make of my life these days
when care is delivered
        in mail and recorded phone calls
without a human face.

2

Don't mean to be silly
        when care is delivered
up in the voice of a women who says
I'm Inder then bla bla
may I help you then helps you
        so you see while on hold
the way the sun throws lacy shadows
on that massive building that sits back
over the cleared spaces
        that once housed workers
and machines and progress but
I don't know
because there is the sun
and Inder saying may I help you.

3

The way the sun throws lacy shadows
through the trees and dresses up my dress
with geometric patterns
     I can't read is the point actually
though I can see
the eyes of men standing
around looking at me
and can read the future
in which the looking becomes mutual
and respectful and
     I don't know
but that a purchase on the real life
so you see while on hold
there is no other important goal
and won't give it more time.

4

Swim suits that look like saucy underwear
and men outfitted in skimpy shorts
with geometric patters
and pockets
as protection for their delicates
lest they become an embarrassment
of a kind never examined
and won't give it more time
     so that I don't know
what to make of a life spent
in attraction on beaches in nothing
but exotic clothing
and wishes for romantic adventure
while gulls mate at the shore.

5

So that a voice speaks out of places
that are sea churned or forest enabled
            or maybe in recognition
of a kind never examined
that there is only place
and pockets
of talk in a real world
since I don't know
about ideas floated on nature's absence
            in the way of desire unspecified
for she who is created by the one
who imagines her figure in garments
applied like those on a paper doll
and I know about that.

6

In the way of desire unspecified
the dance keeps yearning for the dancers
            as does the empty orchestra its fiddles
or maybe it's recognition
that nothing can begin
until those with faces in phones
put down everything
and see a world beyond the ego's hold
or it could be
that nothing can be done for them
but I don't know that's true
            because the light behind their eyes
will look out in spite of them
and all will be bright in their world.

7

Or it could be
that revelers beyond their vision
        are engaged in frivolous activities as
the dance keeps yearning for the dancers
and I don't know exactly what's happening
though I do understand
that something comes next
        as did the lindy the tango and disco
but of course that doesn't say it all
for time's shadow lingers
each time the possibility threatens them
with the world
and someday not too far away
it will be skeletons dancing.

8

To the right are the believers
and to the left those locked into engagement
with the world
        though troubled in ignorance
of calculations I don't know much about
when it comes to a haunting awareness
that something comes next
for all who live on the edge
of governments and their understandings
about everything that alludes them
        as they prelude coming disaster
while those on the right believe them
and to the left is continuing fear
of the rolling thunder.

9

For all who live on the edge
where the township is not managed
         theirs is poverty and freedom
from the daily babble and yet
I don't know
of their understandings
about everything that alludes them
for to be among the privileged
and thus ignorant
is solace
at the edge of somnambulism
where everything seems vaguely possible
as when the moon rises
and the magic carpet carries them away.

10

My underwear is vacant now
and that which was the lurid prize
         for everyman
is solace
as when the moon rises
and I squat upon the beach
to drain my yellow offering like any animal
but I don't know except in sisterhood
will the hammer come down on those others
who in their ignorance
have sinned without know it
         sorrow in the judgment for them
since the hammer is for those
in power and indiscriminate lust.

11

The butcher cuts the meat
that bleeds upon the block
and is presented to the everyman
        for promised satiation
and that which was the lurid prize
so almost sacristan is eaten by those
who in their ignorance
        are smart and sophisticated
though I don't know
since smart is a dime a dozen
but understanding
is the coin of the year
and there is little enough of that
to fill a thimble a shot glass or an wink.

12

The years might limp along
without much understanding
        of the fly on the wall
but understanding
is a record of defeats yet
I don't know
since there is sunshine on the wall
and there is little enough of that
when the fly departs
        her absence in memory
that she is still there
as everything stops for a moment
and those who have departed are back
again under the sun.

13

Outside where I have planted
this woman's mystery garden
          as everything stops for a moment
and I don't know
if the flowers with sister names
who are Rose Jasmine and Lily
will bloom
as much as their namesakes
          in a troubled time
without much understanding
so that a nosegay perched upon my head
is given back as reckoning
and old clothing is worn in the gardening
by those who will alter the world.

14

To again institute that silence provided
so that you see while on hold
          and can read the future
of a kind never examined
that there is only place
or maybe it's recognition
that something comes next
          for all who live on the edge
of their understanding
who in their ignorance
are smart and sophisticated
and those who have departed are back
as everything stops for a moment
and this I know.

After the Storm

They open their coats to reveal
school clothing business attire palates
pajama tops and a women dressed
for an evening out
while those in the wrong shoes
step carefully to avoid the slush
and an old woman my age
is approached by a young man
who lends her his aid
and they limp arm in arm
to the curb.
The storm is over
and all are moving with purpose
heading for imagined adventures.

After the Photograph

Who will have my picture standing
upon art deco
like the one of my parents,
she with a tennis racket along
her shapely leg, he so young yet
presaging his early death?

      She never played that game,
he bit the dust at forty-three,
and I still alive
for the time being at least.

Will the photograph speak to someone
as this one does to me?
Will the sun cast shadows
across my face also?

Young lovers comfortable
in the promise of their futures.
Who might gaze at them and wonder?

After the Concert

Light jackets, silk frocks.
It's spring, late evening.

Couples talk about dinner,
edging those who are fooling around,
laughing and kissing.
          Talk mummers, shoes scrape
on concrete. That's all.

Colored lights
in the buildings across the way.
It has rained,
and the streets glisten.

A plane passes high over head,
and below it
they can hear the distant hum.
It sounds like music.

After Long Silence

Birds chatter and speak to one another
in the park in the night
where small animals are free
of the human condition and can move
out of hiding. All this
while I sleep in the quiet house
and laughter and serious talk
is a ghost all the way to breakfast
after which peace is forgotten
and the energy of the day
speaks out in useless palaver
for ears that have awakened
to begin it all once again.

After the Wedding

The bridesmaids gather together
in a clutch of inward attention, tall and slim,
imagining their futures,
and I find myself lusting for each of them
        which is not a wise thing to be saying
or thinking these days.

So I sidle up to the bride
as if in my presence I can be forgiven,
and the bridegrooms part awkwardly
in their nervousness an ill fitting tuxedos.

"Best wishes," I say, and to the groom
"Congratulations,"
these proper salutations.

There's shrimp on thin sticks, goat cheese,
prosciutto wrapped persimmons,

        and there I am,
lonely for my wife
and our ceremony
as the band plays *I remember you.*

After the Fall

A man on a ladder
that disappears into the clouds.

He looks like a child
at this distance.

Then he reaches the clouds
and enters them.

We can barely see him,
but we see him.

Then comes the decision.
Will he look up and search the sky

for the future, or will he look down
into the vibrant present?

Then he falls.

After Divorce

Two sad sacks,
he with his hands stuck deep in his pockets,
        it's winter, she
in the mink that was his present
twenty years ago.

What should they do,
find another, glory in freedom,
go after that "Self Realization" scam?

The kids were long gone.
        They'd both felt "in a rut,"
and each of them had taken up,
briefly, with another.

Twenty-five years of habits
carved in the brain,
those beautiful children,
a few moments of understanding.

Watch them.
He wears a new suit that doesn't
quite fit, and his mind is always elsewhere.
She's sold her mink, has lost weight,
and is now skinny.

Both are hunched over slightly,
standing or walking.

After Angelica Waiting

She is dressed in her Saturday best
and a little extra in anticipation:
        a few ruffles, possibly ludicrous
given her age.
She's had her hair done, blonde,
and it sparkles.

In restaurants four times
and once for a long walk in the city.
He's a little late;
he never is.

Children in the park across the way,
their grace, their certainty
        in losing time,
as her mind drifts away to other things,
her life, her dead husband

        —and then it's much later,
no more children,
all the stores have closed,
a dark quietness.

She left long ago.

After Longstanding

There was music
having existed or continued
for a long time.
Showers might have fallen on the party,
his retirement, so that
were he to weep at the loss
of everything,
the violins might rise in the strains
of *Some Enchanted Evening.*
But he is dignified
where he stands toying
with his brand-new watch.
He smiles. He is gracious.
His severance check is in his pocket.

After Lingering Illness

It's a summer day
      a few high clouds
soften the sun
that dresses the street
while trees filter and lay thin
shadow ribbons over the houses
mail boxes and cracked sidewalks
as birds sing
and porches hold swings sliders
chairs and tables
each house facing the street
and at number 42
a woman moves quickly down the steps
      into the warm sun
shedding her sick room garments
that fall and ripple
on the bushes and the grass behind her,
as shadow ribbons drape her fresh new body.

After Death

Will there be vapors?
I think I can see through them.

There's a lunch counter,
my wife leaning against it

her figure glimmering white.
I can't stand the longing.

We move toward each other
slowly, stepping through clouds.

How soon might we touch?
The distance between us lengthens,

we're in a movie.
Then there's a fade out

into the final darkness.

Afterwards

We could roll around for a while
then go out and lie naked
on cushions under the bird feeders
        to receive the small offerings
of chickadees and gold finches
that stain our chest with colorful
little dots.

Or maybe we could go out to dinner
and stare at each other lasciviously
across the table.

I might rise and kiss you
in front of everyone.
You might like that.

I've Lost My Whistle

No longer can I call down my birds
or speak Bird.
It's a good thing I have no dog.

A woman stands
        in front of a pet-store window.
There are dogs inside.
Her strident whistle is a siren,
        and the dogs all rush to the window
and press their muzzles against it.

For a taxi, while cooking or idling,
for those dogs. For a beautiful woman passing
        (though I have never done that; well, once).
On your birthday, before dancing, to the sound of singing,
        tune of selling old clothing from a cart.
Of the knife sharpener,
the butcher,
while waiting for the dough to rise.
And of my father, calling us home
        from a night of kick-the-can,
in 1945.

A young man comes down the street whistling a tune
        from the American Song Book,
half forgotten.
I Remember You. He's lost
        in the complicated chord changes,
                and by the time he reaches me
it's a glorious confusion,
very much like Coltrane.

A bartender, a bell-hop, another taxi,
while you work, wetting it,
     Dixie, to start the game,
in the dark, blowing it on some corporate criminal, of a train,
     after love, past the graveyard,
          among ancient ruins,
answering the placid sea.

It's all gone.
I'm an old man counting his losses.
I can no longer accompany their going
with a tune.

Disturbed

1

The genesis of all that rocks the waves
so that the character of flotsam in their curls
when found at surf side
is examined in curiosity and not wonder
  becoming the way of it
those lost chances for the vision
that precedes understanding
so that light coughing in public galleries
where quiet background music is Chopin
while a fog in the civilized head
calls for quiet appreciations
as turbulent oceans on canvases
in elaborate frames
hide their genesis.

2

He remembers the house on the hill
where quiet background music is Chopin
and he is once again in shorts and halter
while mother touches his brow
over and over again
so that he shivers in pleasure and the annoyance
that precedes understanding
as food turns foul in the mouth
where a boy stands in pajamas
ready for bed and aloneness
but for his chicken and rabbit
while the bell in the toy church
rings out death
over and over again.

3

The sea-side marshes are flooded
over and over again
as the oceans deposit their ships' wealth
among weeds and flowers
where fish now struggle in fresh water
and sunset rings out death in the voices
of remaining gulls
who head for their meals or nesting
while among the living
the dead rise up accusingly in memory
in night's shadows in lamp light
and guilt foolishly comes to roost
as food turns foul in the mouth
of those who feed upon death.

4

But now the mother is dead
and he is forty-three
in night's shadows in lamp light
whereupon a table holds his whiskey
that he might be oiled for reading
these books of those who feed upon death
in a history before his own
while among the living
politics rages
and there is no power in those
caught up in the maelstrom
as the dead rock in somebody's paradise
while hell is only a vague promise in books
as he raises his glass.

5

Caught up in the maelstrom
and white clouds hung low
over the bay's unshadowed majesty
the bait fish rose turbulent to the surface
in futile escape from the death below
while gulls squawked in the air
announcing death's presence
a feast for the fishermen who
        in this sad half natural cycle
gathered on waves in aggressive circles
again and again in view
of that house on the hill now vacant
as the sea held sway as witness
in a history before his own.

6

In futile escape from the death below
there are turbulent explorations
        and wet hair under his arms
in Chet Baker's honey in the living-room
where there are surf-stones
numbered and dated
in artistic piles that are sea tossed
and a messy abstract hung on the wall
in this sad half natural cycle
their juicy pleasures
and he knows she has him
        locked away from his taste
as clay animals strut on the mantle
and a shorn Poodle licks away at his toes.

7

Numbered and dated
the ships march out across the Atlantic
invisible beyond sight from the yearning shore
where there are surf-stones
and the mysteries inside the ships
are sea tossed
and mystery is memory
as much as the shuffling cargo
is scuttling towards its own future
while this drama's story
might reach out and touch the ships
even as the sea-side watchers
picnic or lie in the sun
and take delight in the empty waves.

8

This is about a man who returns
to the beach of his childhood at sixty-seven
where there are numbered stones
        scattered in the sand
and the vacant house on the hill
is the dead past
and about a confusion of papers
on a desk where he spends his life
in the construction of other lives
        so that all else becomes illusion
and he might think of the grave yard
as he imagines his mother
in the house on the hill above
gazing at the sea through windows.

9

And behind his mother's face
is the face of the wife that has joined her
so that all else becomes illusion
as he whittles away at the days
a glass of bourbon
among the scatter of papers on the desk
where time meanders
in the construction of other lives
while the body confronts its slow collapse
and he can hardly rise to reach his pencil
though he is strong enough
to confront his reading
and the confusion of dead characters
in the book beside the bourbon.

10

And in the book a man travels
into various tortured circumstances
        sets off to sail upon a distant sea
and discovers the rotting cargo
where time meanders
while paragraphs are both repeated
and created in his mind
at the edge of sleep
so that all else becomes illusion
and the cargo in his head
becomes the story
of loss and pathological longing
that lingers in the sleeper's imagination
as the book ridicules the reader.

11

And yet he is forced to the stories
that he has created
and the ones still to be brought
to a kind of life that is not life
though in time there will be an ending
and the cargo in the head will rot
as the story teller becomes the story
of loss and pathological longing
but for the bourbon
that sits among papers
and brings an appropriate dullness
to the one who is dealing in machination
as the desk is facing the window
through which the sea is unconcerned.

12

Once again the sea confronts the story
with disregard
as the sailor unfurls his canvas
upon which no words are written
and the bluefish school
at the ankles of the oyster picker
and the surf licks the toes
of the beautiful maidens
while far out and beyond vision
whales breach and blow
in those hours of the day
when the sea is placid
and holds their massive bodies
gently caressing them.

13

And so does he come to be eighty
and becomes the story
of a teller of limited ability
who nevertheless tells his stories
here on the Cape in May and sunlight
        where silence is a reminder
that the time is short
and all the while I am leaving
my bed at 4 a.m.
drinking coffee and remembering
that I love that past
in which I meet my people once again
admire their power in the memory
and write about them.

14

The sea is calm tonight
as seen from his window
and there are soft lights in fog
in the town cut at the hook
        and people might be dancing there
or sitting at restaurant table
overlooking the placid waters
while house lights blink
along the curve of shore
and motors on the highway are trivial
as the fenders are still
at the gunwales of boats at the dock
yet the distance between us as always
is the wild uninterested sea.

A Wink and a Nod

A hundred days of solitude
and you
      in memory standing
in your thoughtful beauty
at the bed side
even as my teeth fall out
and there's macular degeneration.
      I'm not really complaining,
just thought I'd mention it.

These rooms hold the desire
not the objects in them
but pathways
      where we followed or led one another
where we pulled out our chairs for dinner
and sat down facing each other
in the sinking sun.

      And I'm touching the walls
the handles on the kitchen cabinets
the pathway leading to the glass table
its smooth beveled edge
and dusty surface.

Solitude is not aloneness.
      There you are,
and I've been thinking about our adventure
at the gym.

You were sweating. Even your hair was soaked. You lifted for ten
minutes more, grunting and gasping, then you dropped the bar
with a thud, and we went home.

This didn't happened of course,
this imagining from remembered gestures,
and maybe it's a silly little joke.

      But we were silly, sometimes,
and we joked about a lot of things.
You were not powerful in your body.
It was your mind, your humor,
and my passion for them.

Sit down. Have a drink.
Be here.

I have your pictures, eternal
as these memories
haunt, yet sometimes please,
and you lost the car keys near the end.

      Our passages are worn into the rugs.
I might have winked at you at the gym.
You might have nodded in response.

A hundred ghosts, a half century.
Soon I too
go down.

Child Lost in the Forest

1

She is dressed in shorts
and a blouse
        inappropriate
here among the shadows
cast down from dark trees.

It's late afternoon
and she is eight years old
and a little cold.

Where is my mother she whispers
her chin sunk into ruffles
at her throat.

She has been lost for a whole day.
What can she do?

Her hair is blond and long
and it falls to her shoulders
in golden ringlets.

2

The first night she slept
in a bed made of fallen pine boughs.
They were itchy and she was cold.

She was hungry.
The red berries on the bushes
        were bitter and she spat them out,
and she didn't trust the mushrooms.

It is midday
and she is still wandering around
        looking for something to do.
Her bed is made
and she has found a stump for a seat.

She would wander off
        in search of a way back
to somewhere
but she fears losing the world
she now inhabits.

Look at her,
eight years old, thin
as a stick.

3

What happens now?
   The sun is sinking and she knows
she'll be staying there for another night.
         "Helga!" they'll call out,
seeing her, or hearing her,
as they emerge from the trees.

But that's latter.
She's hungry
and she must find food.

She searches the woods close by
and comes upon amaranth.
Her pink blouse is soiled,
      her white tennis shoes,
her shorts.
There are scratches on her bare legs.
She doesn't care.

She lays her foods out
      on the tall stump,
asparagus to the left, amaranth on the right
and chicory flowers for a garnish.

   It looks like a proper lunch,
and she jabs at the food with a sharp stick,
but its evening now
and the shadows turn her stump
into a table in a nightclub.

She better eat, then get to bed.
Animals are beginning to sound off.

4

She wakes in the morning
eats fireweed
        then pees among the trees.
Then she goes to her pine bed
and arranged the boughs so they look right.
She takes her place on the stump.

They come,
her stern father from the left,
dressed in conventional woods-wear,
        her mother clomping in from the right.
And her dour sisters and brother
and those from the village
enlisted for the search.

Her family stands to the side
while others laugh and chatter.
        And there are cameras and phones
and hand movies being made.

And there she is
        on her stump
among streamers and flags and dancers,
and she lifts the edge of her shorts
and slices her thin leg
with the sharp stick.

The last rays of the sun
wash geometric figures through her hair
and on her face and soiled blouse.
Blood drips from the wound.

Alone
in the maelstrom.

Etudes   —*for Miriam, in memory*

1

The impressions of bodies in the chairs
and couches in the living room
the scent of them absent
        while the land seen through
the window and the sea
remain constant
as your face in shadow
lingers to the sides of faces
I talk to smiling
unaware
yet sure in the third Irish and water
your face my compass
as conversation rots in the mouth
until the party's over.

2

Unaccounted for at sunset's prelude
in the window and the sea
beyond which night Paris still glimmers
        in our absence
in memory at least walking at the *Seine's* side
gazing at those who are young
as we grow older
and I am left only with thoughts
        of you buying *saucisson sec*
a *baguette* and wine for a picnic
the four of us together on grass in a park
who are now only one
        this self without lover and friends
as conversation rots in the mouth.

3

After a night of calm adventure
        monopoly and marijuana
the house in which we lived
container of a past was
in our absence
locked tight in memory
and I am left only with thoughts
of passion's last meal
        as you began to drift away
and for a while I was with you
lagging behind
summer fall and the last winter
in which you called me your father
mother and good friend.

4

Each day the breath of winter's sadness
locked tight in memory
of the last turkey you could not see
        as I forced your vision
hopelessly
while winter fell in crystal snow
lagging behind
the very thought of you twisted
until I had no name but care
        and in the fluid's flood
of cleaning and tucking in
what chance did I have
but lifting a soup spoon to your lips
the flavors of our final connections.

5

To breath in memories of sin
and in the fluid's flood
      to mark down passages in time
but yet to find the beauty in the sinister
of what has befallen
after hours and days passing in notice
so that our time together
      be fresh as roses in blossom
even as those flowers wilt away
hopelessly
and time becomes a measure of dessication
here where I am standing and you are sitting
leaning your head against my hip
as we contemplate nothing.

6

Our house close to the rambling of the sea
that seems constant witness
      of what has befallen
yet beckons us to the self's exit into a clarity
down wind from transpired
difficulties
and you my love were harbinger
      of what I would be following
so that our time together
in those last days
became eternal in a present moment
that remains still in memory
as if a photograph in constant motion
empty of tears shuddering and regrets.

7

As the literal was transcribed
and the story arrived at midpoint
        we found ourselves in a new city
pining for those earlier days
in which what's left behind is prelude
that remains still in memory
of all those figures haunting us
until in darkness and this city's lights
        were harbingers
of what I would be following
into these calm adventures
just the two of us
and dare I speak of loving you
which is inadequate.

8

Things that were there are no longer there
as when in the old kitchen
        I wonder why I'm here
until in darkness and this city's lights
all becomes apparent
in your recipes and utensils
        your hands in the rubber gloves
which is inadequate
and is not you
your mind and shoulders and your smile
in thoughts of you coming unbidden
without any effort
so that here you are not in thought but in vision
and here I am the lonely boy.

9

I wonder why I'm here
        after rage in your sickness
sitting in this whicker chair
a purchase agreed upon
well before construction of this interior
house world done
        without any effort
so that gatherings of objects might define
a marriage in eclecticism and did
even as water on oil
and after these endings that left all beginnings
two became one
as in darkness before lamps were lit
to reveal these empty spaces.

10

My days now in oblivion
of useless meandering in the leavings
        even as water on oil
allows no emulsion
and the now is only embarrassment
as in darkness before lamps were lit
        to reveal the shadow of your smile
to the sides of faces engaged in conversations
I take little part in
        telling jokes that are a mask
and when the party is over and your face
has faded for a while
I take momentary pleasures while cleaning up
until your face appears again and I am lost.

11

When you showed me the photographs
taken when you were younger
I remarked on your beauty
        though beauty is in the eye of the beholder
and I don't believe that
since I saw your spirit in you as something
I take little part in
believing in your autonomy even when the past
has faded for a while
though in the clutch of self pity
        that is my nature these days
who once was no more than a late adolescent
shrugging into your presence
full of frustrated desire.

12

The mind in a caravan of lost opportunities
that is my nature these days
even as I try to catch up to your ashes
        and scatter my own above you
in a time slowly approaching
and I don't believe that
heavenly choirs will attend us
        even as relatives morn
until they too join us
and time stops
though in the meantime let me go on
even in this oblivion
        where angels parade in old paintings
and words ride into a void.

13

In a time slowly approaching
where memory ends
　　　and your favorite music
is defiled in the ears of the living
though you would give it kindly and with a smile
I can still see
　　　even in this oblivion
where days are counted toward an ending
that will gain us nothing
since your spark of life has been extinguished
leaving this other half
　　　to stand beside the sedum
given to you by our cleaning lady
called live forever.

14

As conversation rots in the mouth
unaccounted for at sunset's prelude
of passions last meal
　　　while winter fell in crystal snow
and time becomes a measure of dessication
yet beckons us to the self's exit into a clarity
　　　until in darkness and this city's lights
so that here you are not in thought but in vision
well before construction of this interior
and the now is only embarrassment
though in the clutch of self pity
　　　that is my nature these days
since your spark of life has been extinguished
and I can only say goodbye.

That Way

The kids, my love, are drawing circles in the sand.
How simple their devices,
a stick, laughter, some imagination.
        These certain children are just.
Their circles are not.

No sand in the inland summer,
so jumping games,
something we didn't get around to,
though at times, in your presence,
I might have jumped for joy.

You are gone.
The circles have given in to the tide.
The children are gone.
There's a dear woman beside me.
She doesn't know what I'm thinking:

        summer on Bonaire.
The fruit boat in from Venezuela.
You are delighted.
That night, in our dark hut,
iguanas scratched on the tin roof.

How foolish to consider
these foolish things:
        your wedding dress in the closet,
still, after forty-nine years. A hat and a scarf,
a favored coat.
I could see you in them, wearing them all.

Yet I am not alone in my madness.
Memory: there you are
        in my silly construction,
a wooden hand and a foot,
the way, in illness, you cared for me
hand and foot.

And just walking down the street together,
side by side, not holding hands,
your awareness
of everything: fabrics, buildings and blown leaves,
        all the way to the earth's rotation.
And where you stood was center

                        and gravity. What chance did I have?
One evening in darkness: your hair,
        the tilt of your head, that little light.
You are reading, and from my vantage
you are viewed only in silhouette.

These impossible images, fixed on film
        in some kind of photography
and quite dead.
Let me listen to your music,
keep you alive
that way.

On a forthright spring afternoon,
surrounded by the wonder of her flowers,
and still stunned,
it came to me:
        I had not thought of you
in two long days.

The Meal

Something out of the corner of the eye
or in the eye;
        something discovered in passing
[not nous in the passage]
within time spent in the concrete [a ladle,
a knife], recipes
fallen down from a bookcase.

The meal of the day is flanken:
        [Put meat in. And cover with water
or a little more than cover.]
blessings on the animal's flesh treated
so well in the preparation.
            And carrots in the corner of the eye
in time spent in the passage. And dumplings
formed carefully in the hands.
[Cook until meat
falls from bones. Constant skimming.]

And of course time passes in the treating
        [turnips in the corner of the eye
ripening]; remains of the animal passes
to a final destination
            [location possibly noted
in new growth], and we have come through
yet again.
        [Put carrots and dumplings in. Continue
until all is ready.]

Something in the corner of knowledge
        [in the nose in the passage],
which is not knowledge

[in the great passage] formed
carefully in the hands, but flesh of the animal
treated to carrots and destination
        [the only passage], through yet again
to rise up in the new growth
in the garden [eggplant,
                basil and broccoli],
something out of the corner of the eye,
received in the eye
[the nose].

Blood of the passage in constant skimming
which is not nous but coming through
        yet again partially changed
until all is ready. Something [a side dish,
wine, a ladle] in a corner in living,
a woman's knife and dumplings.

The meal of the days is discovered
        in the corner of the eye's passage,
in the flesh heated to release scent
                of garlic for the nose
[in the corner where a woman stands],
        for the palm cupping the ear
to the bubble
[until the meat falls]
which is not skimming knowledge.

Fallen down from a bookcase,
        ingredients of the careful lesson
[a recipe, a code, a knife]
gathered up from the floor of the dead
                [location possibly noted]
given back into the corner of the eye,

not nous in the passage.
Seltzer on the table, a ladle, elbows,
compliments to the chef
        [into a fanfare], treated
to carrots and destination.

And of course time passes
        in time spent in the passage,
a simmer in the corner of the eye fallen
down from a counter,
recipes from a bookcase
there on the floor of the dead.
                Flesh of the beast as a burnt patient
the woman is carefully nursing,
        down in the scent of garlic,
anticipated skimming,
putting the meat in [casual sacrament]
out of the corner of the eye, caught
        partially changed
in the great passage [the only passage].
Cook until meat falls from bones,
until carrots grow vibrantly
dark orange color
        in time spent in the concrete
[wound that will not heal].

Yet again in the conversation
                [location possibly noted]
of new growth in the corner of the eye,
sacrament of the animal's passage
        within skimming of destinations
[garlic, a ladle, a knife],
fanfare of compliments
for the chef's knowledge [but not nous]
of blood breathing

in the nose in the passage
[desire for reversal of fortune]
        in the nose in the passage
of blood breathing
for the chef's knowledge [but not fallen]
                fanfare of compliments
[up from the floor of the dead]
within skimming for destinations,
        sacrament of the animal's passage
of new growth
in the corner of the eye
in a garden of eggplant and tomato
                [location possibly noted]
yet again in the conversation;
the meat falls down from the bones,
carrots grow vibrantly
dark orange color
        [the wound that will not heal]
in time spent in the concrete.

Out of the corner of the eye caught
putting the meat in [casual sacrament],
in the great passage
        the woman is carefully nursing
flesh of the beast as a burnt patient
there on the floor of the dead
recipe from a bookcase,
a ladle in the corner of the ear fallen
        in time spent in the passage,
[the meal of the day is discovered]
and of course time passes
until all is ready.

[Flanken. Carrots and dumplings.
        Blessings on the animal's flesh

treated so well in the preparation
  and on the woman's hands in the corner,
a sacrament
fallen down among recipes from a bookcase,
the floor of the dead littered
  in the great passage] The only passage.
[Ingredients of the careful lesson,
a conversation
  in the concrete, which is not knowledge.

Blood of the passage in constant skimming
of the meat put into a simmer
on the passage through
  to a final destination,
location possibly noted
in new growth.] And we have come
into the corner of the eye yet again,
partially changed.
Desire for reversal of passage
up from the corner of the eye's recipe
[casual sacrament],
  not fallen discovery. The floor of the dead
grows vibrant, garlic, a knife, a ladle,
   ingredients of the conversation,
a fanfare: careful lesson [location
possibly noted] in new growth.

  And we have come through yet again.
Flanken. Seltzer on the table, elbows, a woman
brushing the floor of the skimming.
  Off in a corner of the eye,
a bouquet of carnations, a pot, a ladle;
the wine blood is breathing.
  It's getting late; time passes.
Let us begin the meal.